WHAT HANDS CAN DO !

A SONG ABOUT FRIENDSHIP

By VITA JIMÉNEZ

Illustrations by JANET CHEESEMAN

Music by MARK OBLINGER

CANTATA
LEARNING

WWW.CANTATALEARNING.COM

CANTATA LEARNING

Published by Cantata Learning
1710 Roe Crest Drive
North Mankato, MN 56003
www.cantatalearning.com

A note to educators and librarians from the publisher: Cantata Learning has provided the following data to assist in book processing and suggested use of Cantata Learning product.

Publisher's Cataloging-in-Publication Data
Prepared by Librarian Consultant: Ann-Marie Begnaud
Library of Congress Control Number: 2016938069
    What Hands Can Do! : A Song about Friendship
    Series: Me, My Friends, My Community
    By Vita Jiménez
    Illustrations by Janet Cheeseman
    Music by Mark Oblinger
    Summary: Positive, upbeat lyrics and colorful illustrations teach children that hands can do many good things, from making a delicious pie to helping someone after they fall.
    ISBN: 978-1-63290-780-6 (library binding/CD)
Suggested Dewey and Subject Headings:
    Dewey: E 612.9
    LCSH Subject Headings: Hand – Utilization – Juvenile literature. | Helping behavior – Juvenile literature. | Hand – Utilization – Songs and music – Texts. | Helping behavior – Songs and music – Texts. | Hand – Utilization – Juvenile sound recordings. | Helping behavior – Juvenile sound recordings.
    Sears Subject Headings: Human body. | Helping behavior. | School songbooks. | Children's songs. | Rock music.
    BISAC Subject Headings: JUVENILE NONFICTION / Concepts / Body. | JUVENILE NONFICTION / Music / Songbooks. | JUVENILE NONFICTION / Social Topics / Friendship.

Book design and art direction: Tim Palin Creative
Editorial direction: Flat Sole Studio
Music direction: Elizabeth Draper
Music written and produced by Mark Oblinger

Printed in the United States of America in North Mankato, Minnesota.
072017   0367CGF17

ACCESS THE MUSIC!

SCAN CODE WITH MOBILE APP

CANTATALEARNING.COM

TIPS TO SUPPORT LITERACY AT HOME

WHY READING AND SINGING WITH YOUR CHILD IS SO IMPORTANT

Daily reading with your child leads to increased academic achievement. Music and songs, specifically rhyming songs, are a fun and easy way to build early literacy and language development. Music skills correlate significantly with both phonological awareness and reading development. Singing helps build vocabulary and speech development. And reading and appreciating music together is a wonderful way to strengthen your relationship.

READ AND SING EVERY DAY!

TIPS FOR USING CANTATA LEARNING BOOKS AND SONGS DURING YOUR DAILY STORY TIME

1. As you sing and read, point out the different words on the page that rhyme. Suggest other words that rhyme.

2. Memorize simple rhymes such as Itsy Bitsy Spider and sing them together. This encourages comprehension skills and early literacy skills.

3. Use the questions in the back of each book to guide your singing and storytelling.

4. Read the included sheet music with your child while you listen to the song. How do the music notes correlate to the words of the song?

5. Sing along on the go and at home. Access music by scanning the QR code on each Cantata book. You can also stream or download the music for free to your computer, smartphone, or mobile device.

Devoting time to daily reading shows that you are available for your child. Together, you are building language, literacy, and listening skills.

Have fun reading and singing!

Our hands are very special. They help us do almost everything. We use our hands to get ready for school, to open a door, and to carry books. We can also use our hands to help others, show **respect**, and let people know how much we care.

Now turn the page and sing along about your special hands!

SCHOOL BUS

Hands can throw a ball
or hold a bat.
They know just when to clap, clap, clap.

Hands are special.
Hands are fun.

Hands are part
of everyone!

Hands can help you up
if you fall down.

Hands can help you
around your town.

Hands can paint
or help you write.

Hands can even
fly a kite.

Hands can button
or help you tie.

Hands can make
an apple pie.

Hands can plant
and water a tree.

Hands can **recycle**
the **trash**, you see.

Hands are special.
Hands are fun.

Hands are part
of everyone!

Hands can pick things up
or put them down.

Hands can build
a brand new town.

Hands can talk.
Hands can play.

We use hands
every day!

Hands are special.
Hands are fun.

Hands are part
of everyone!

Hands are special.
Hands are fun.

Hands are part
of everyone!

SONG LYRICS
What Hands Can Do!

Hands can throw a ball
or hold a bat.
They know just when
to clap, clap, clap.

Hands are special.
Hands are fun.
Hands are part
of everyone!

Hands can help you up
if you fall down.
Hands can help you
around your town.

Hands can paint
or help you write.
Hands can even
fly a kite.

Hands can button
or help you tie.
Hands can make
an apple pie.

Hands can plant
and water a tree.
Hands can recycle
the trash, you see.

Hands are special.
Hands are fun.
Hands are part
of everyone!

Hands can pick things up
or put them down.
Hands can build
a brand new town.

Hands can talk.
Hands can play.
We use hands
every day!

Hands are special.
Hands are fun.
Hands are part
of everyone!

Hands are special.
Hands are fun.
Hands are part
of everyone!

What Hands Can Do!

Rock and Roll
Mark Oblinger

Verse

G · C · D · G

1. Hands can throw a ball or hold a bat. They know just when to clap, clap, clap.

Chorus

Emin7 · C#dim · D7 · G

Hands are spe - cial. Hands are fun. Hands are part of eve - ry - one!

Interlude

G · C#dim · D7 · G

Verse 2
Hands can help you up
if you fall down.
Hands can help you
around your town.

Interlude

Verse 3
Hands can paint
or help you write.
Hands can even
fly a kite.

Interlude

Verse 4
Hands can button
or help you tie.
Hands can make
an apple pie.

Interlude

Verse 5
Hands can plant
and water a tree.
Hands can recycle
the trash, you see.

Chorus

Interlude

Verse 6
Hands can pick things up
or put them down.
Hands can build
a brand new town.

Interlude

Verse 7
Hands can talk.
Hands can play.
We use hands
every day!

Interlude

Chorus (x2)

Outro

G · C#dim · D7 · G

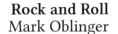
23

GLOSSARY

respect—a way of treating people in a kind way

recycle—to use something again

trash—things that are no longer useful and have been thrown away

GUIDED READING ACTIVITIES

1. Who do you help with your hands? Think of three ways you can use your hands to help others.

2. Imagine what life would be like without hands. What things wouldn't you be able to do? What things could you find another way to do?

3. Draw a picture of your favorite way to help others.

TO LEARN MORE

Higgins, Melissa. *I Am Respectful*. North Mankato, MN: Capstone, 2014.

Parker, Victoria. *Helping in the Community*. North Mankato, MN: Heinemann-Raintree, 2012.

Paul, Miranda. *Whose Hands Are These? A Community Helper Guessing Book*. Minneapolis: Millbrook Press, 2016.

Preus, Janet. *People Who Help in My Neighborhood*. North Mankato, MN: Cantata Learning. 2016.